Dorchester to Aylmer Ontario in Colour Photos, Saving Our History One Photo at a Time

I0484515

Photography
by Barbara Raué
2014

Series Name:
Cruising Ontario

Book 77: Dorchester to Aylmer

Cover photo: 4026 Hamilton Road, Dorchester

Series Name: Cruising Ontario
Saving Our History One Photo at a Time

Other Books by Barbara Raue

Coins of Gold

Arrows, Indians and Love

The Life and Times of Barbara
Volume 1: Inventions That Have Enhanced My Life
Volume 2: Entertainment That I Have Enjoyed
Volume 3: East Coast Trips
Volume 4: Olympics Have Always Intrigued Me
Volume 5: Wonders of the World
Volume 6: Caribbean Cruises We Have Enjoyed
Volume 7: Animals
Volume 8: Storms and Other Major Disasters in My Lifetime
Volume 9: Wars, Terrorist Attacks and Major Disasters

The Cromwell Family Book

Laura Secord Discovered

Visit Barbara's website to view all of her books
http://barbararaue.ca

Thames Centre is a municipality in Middlesex County located in southwestern Ontario a few kilometres east of London. Communities in the township include: Avon, Belton, Cherry Grove, Crampton, Cobble Hill, Derwent, Devizes, **Dorchester**, Evelyn, Fanshawe Lake, Friendly Corners, Gladstone, **Harrietsville**, Kelly Station, **Mossley**, Nilestown, Oliver, Putnam, Salmonville, Silvermoon, Thorndale, Three Bridges, and Wellburn. **Dorchester** is the residential and commercial core of the township.

Mossley

Until 1840 the Mossley area was an untouched wilderness of pines, maples, and beeches. The first settlers from England, Scotland, Ireland and Wales worked hard to clear the land for farming. They came with few tools but great hope for a better way of life, and they prospered. In the 1800s this area was known simply as "The Corners". In 1865 John Henry Amos opened a general store and was the first postmaster. The name Mossley was chosen from two family names, the Mossips and the Lees. Mossley had a hotel, a cheese factory, a harness repair shop, and there were dressmakers and music teachers.

Malahide Township was named for Malahide Castle in Malahide, Ireland, birthplace of land grant administrator Colonel Thomas Talbot in 1810. The township comprises the communities of Candyville, Crossley-Hunter, Copenhagen, Dunboyne, Fairview, Glencolin, Grovesend, Jaffa, Kingsmill, Lakeview, Little Aylmer, Luton, **Lyons**, Mile Corner, Mount Salem, Mount Vernon, Ormond Beach, Orwell, **Port Bruce**, Seville, Springfield, Summers Corners and Waneeta Beach.

Table of Contents

Dorchester

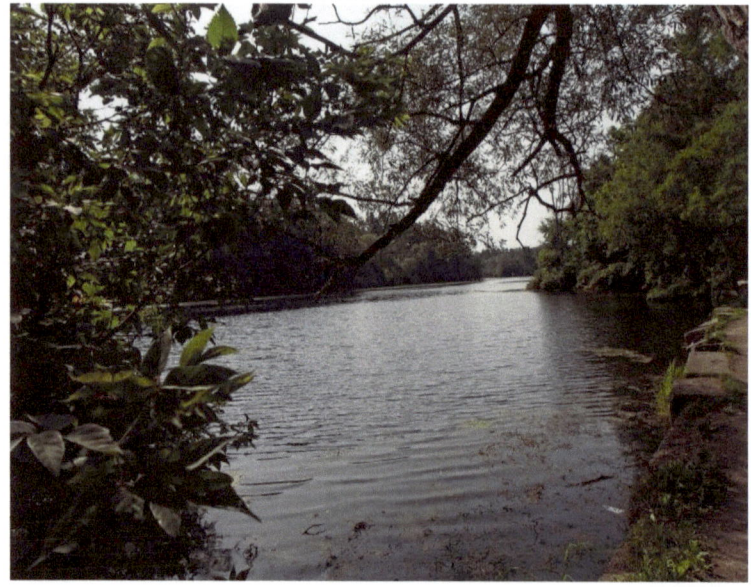

Dorchester Mill Pond

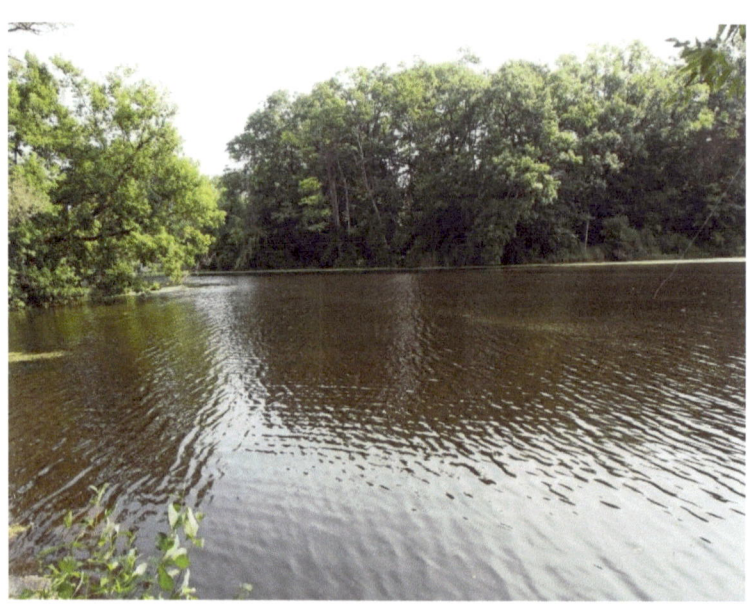

The Neutral Indians, an important confederation of Iroquoian tribes, kept semi-permanent settlements on the banks of the Mill Pond. Hamilton Road was formerly a local trail leading from Lake Ontario to the river crossing at Detroit. The dam and mill were built well before 1810. The Mill Pond is well known for its cedar and white pine with many of its trees being floated down the river to be used in the construction of settlements in Detroit. The land on which the dam now sits was owned by William Cartwright in 1828. Probably a saw mill was built here. Mr. Cartwright established the first grist mill in Dorchester.

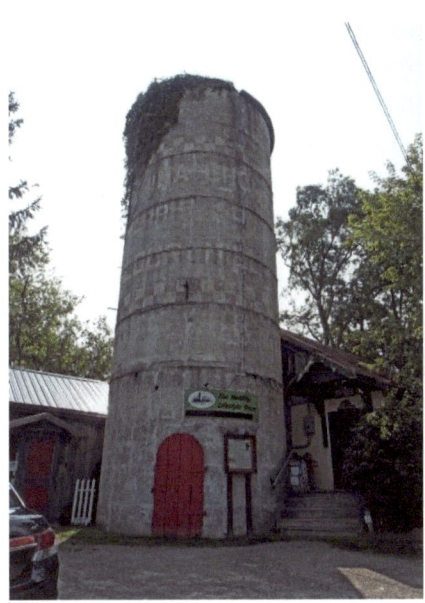 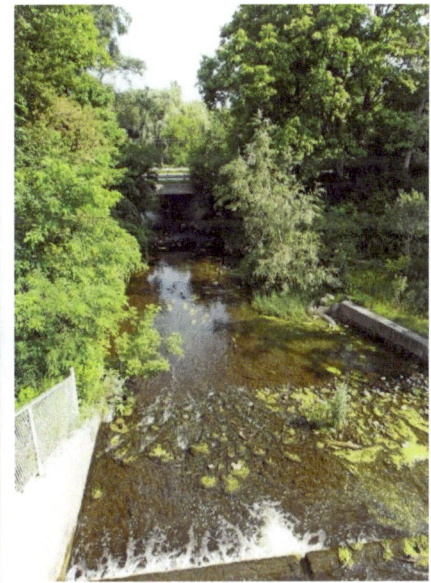

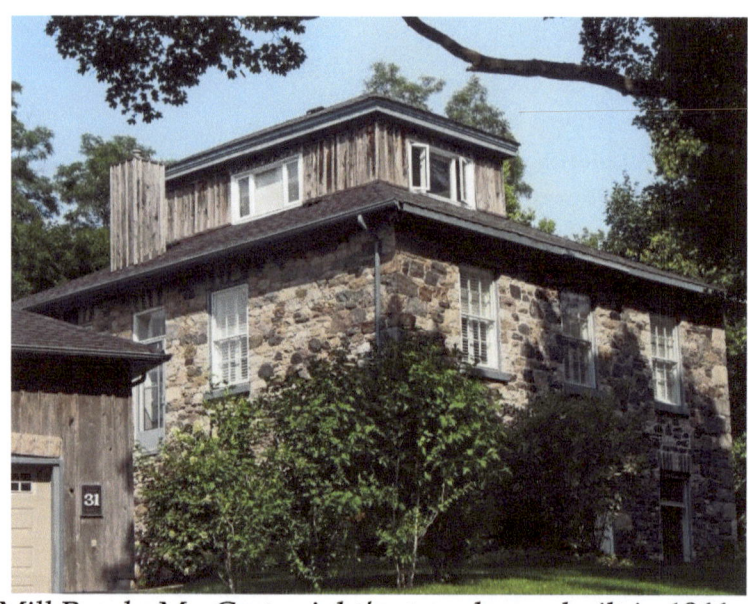

31 Mill Road - Mr. Cartwright's stone house built in 1866 with river and field stones with eighteen inch thick walls – Georgian style. There are ten main rooms. There is a "widow's walk" or belvedere on the roof with a view of the river from windows on all four sides.

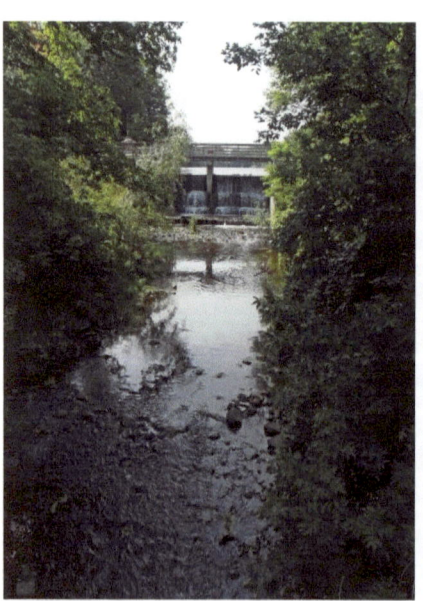
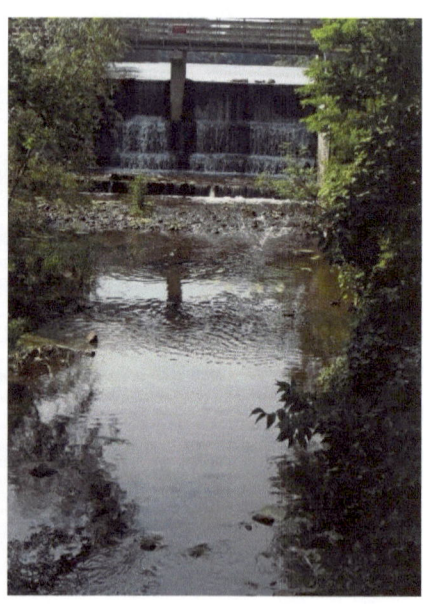

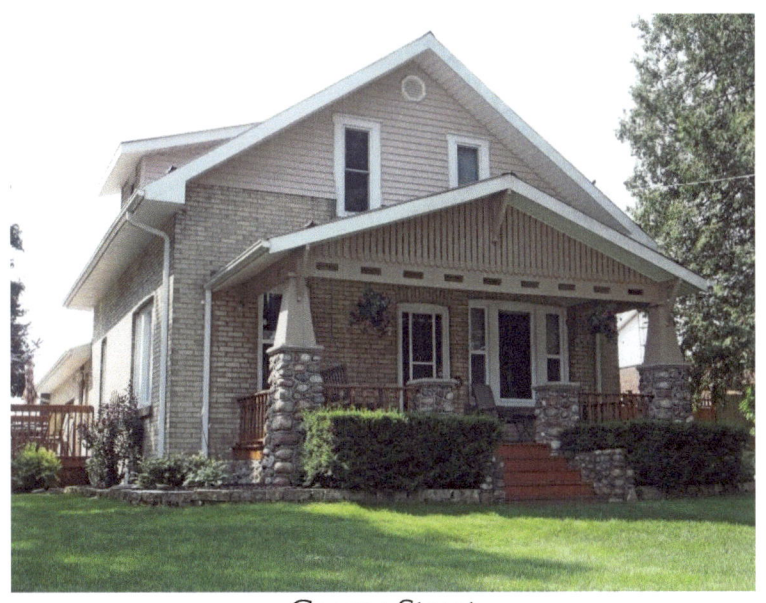

George Street

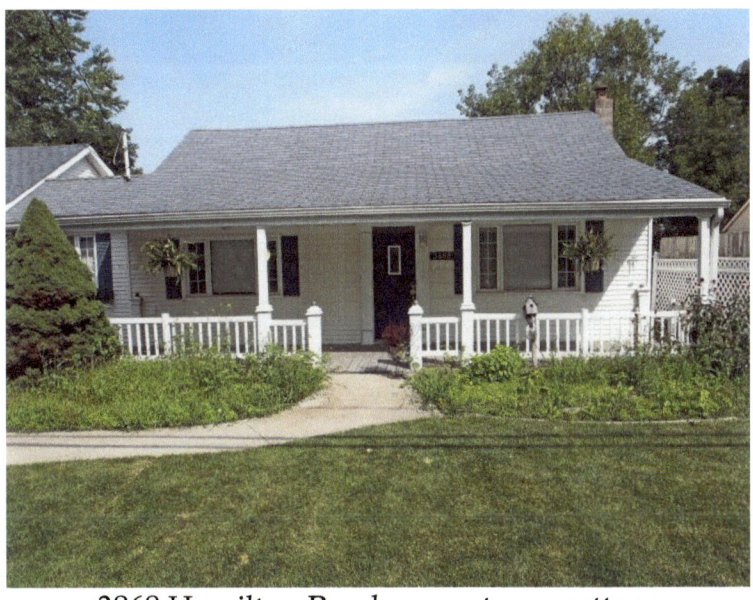

3868 Hamilton Road – one storey cottage

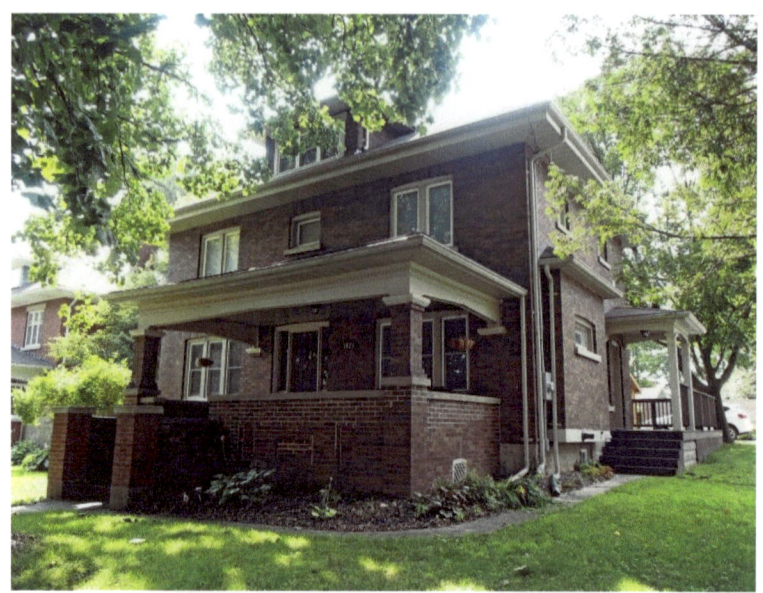

3925 Hamilton Road – Italianate, dormer in attic

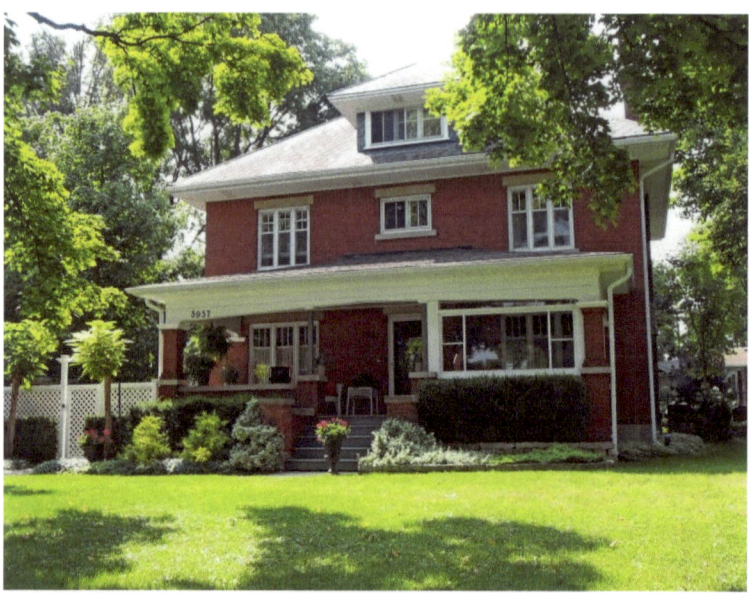

3937 Hamilton Road – Italianate, dormer in attic

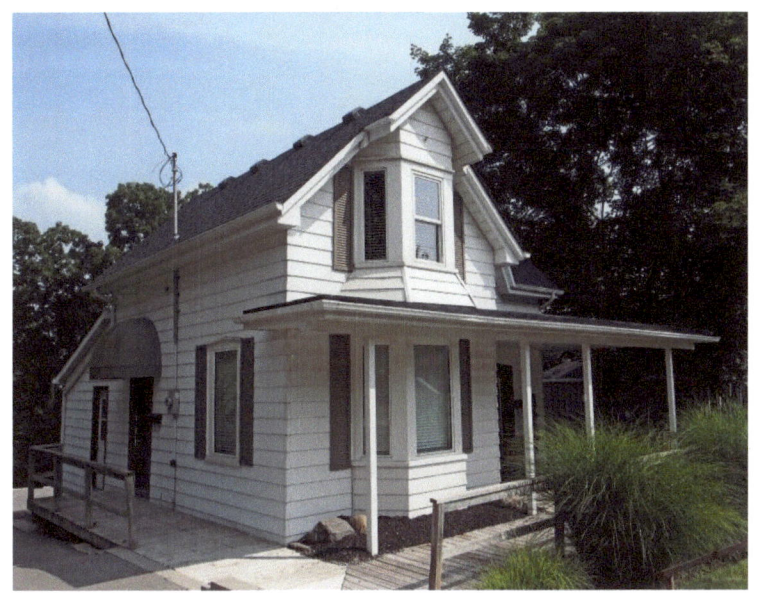

3936 Hamilton Road – Gothic Revival

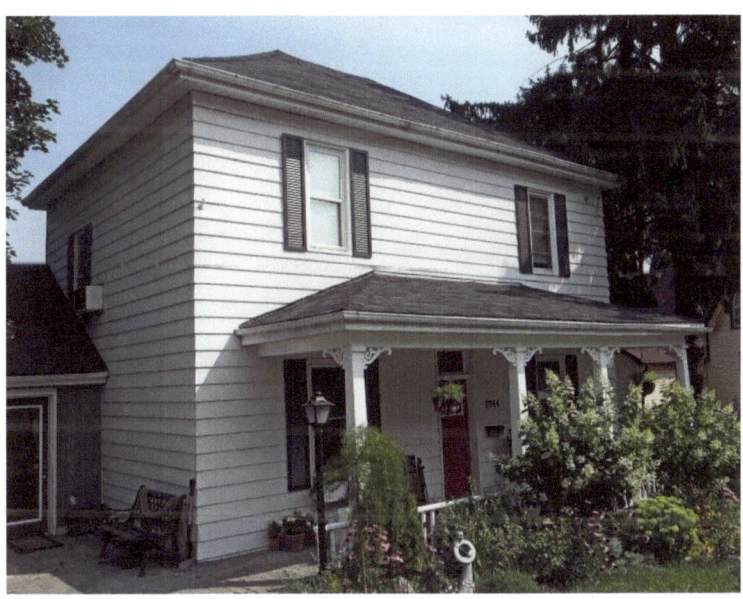

3944 Hamilton Road – Italianate, hipped roof

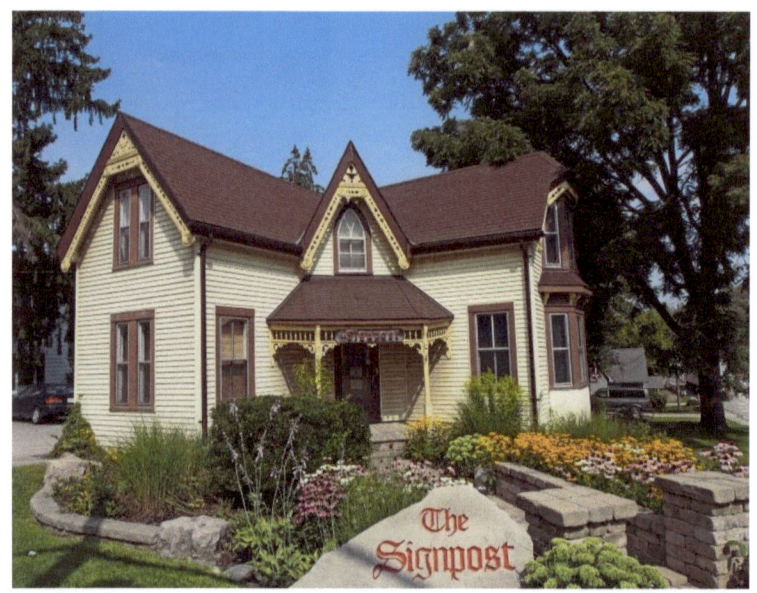

15 Bridge Street – The Signpost – Gothic Revival, Vergeboard trim on gables

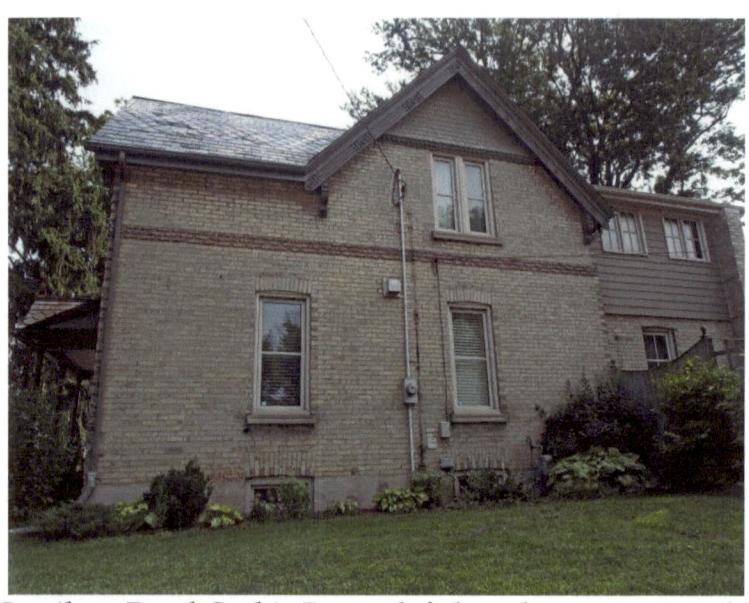

Hamilton Road Gothic Revival, fish scale pattern in gable

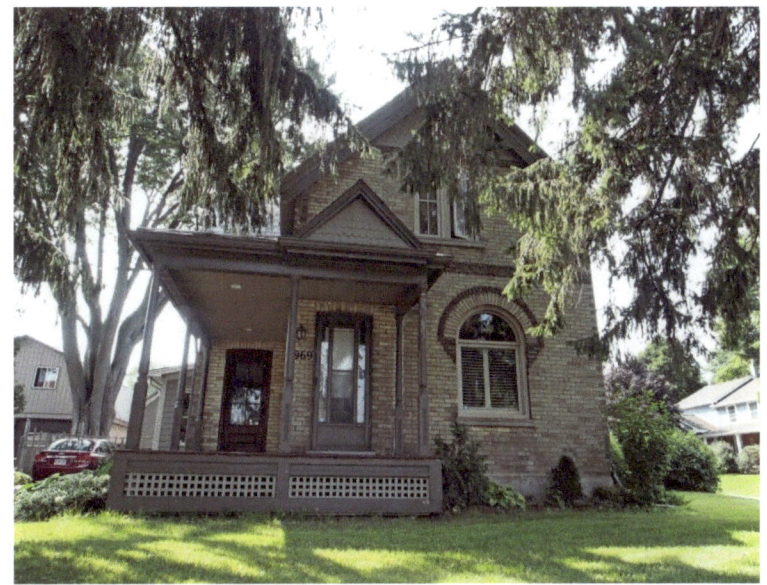

3969 Hamilton Road – Gothic Revival, Romanesque style
window arch, pediment above door

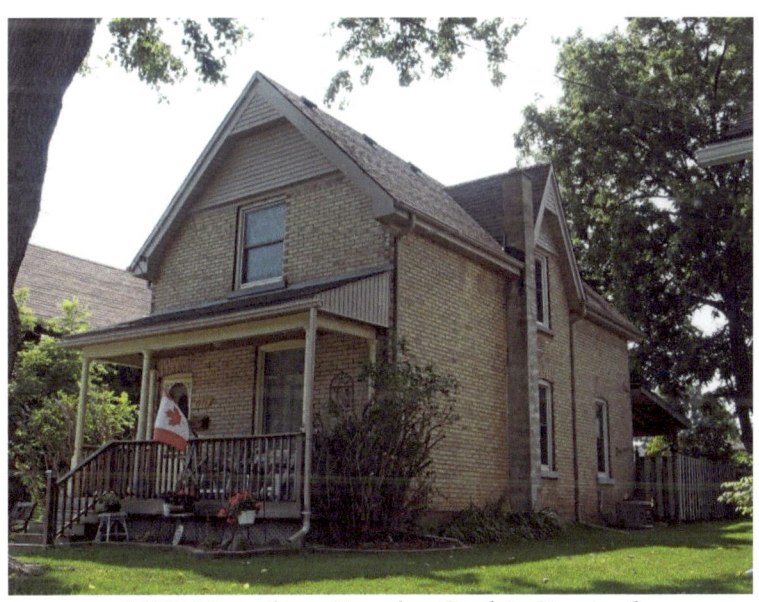

3979 Hamilton Road – Gothic Revival

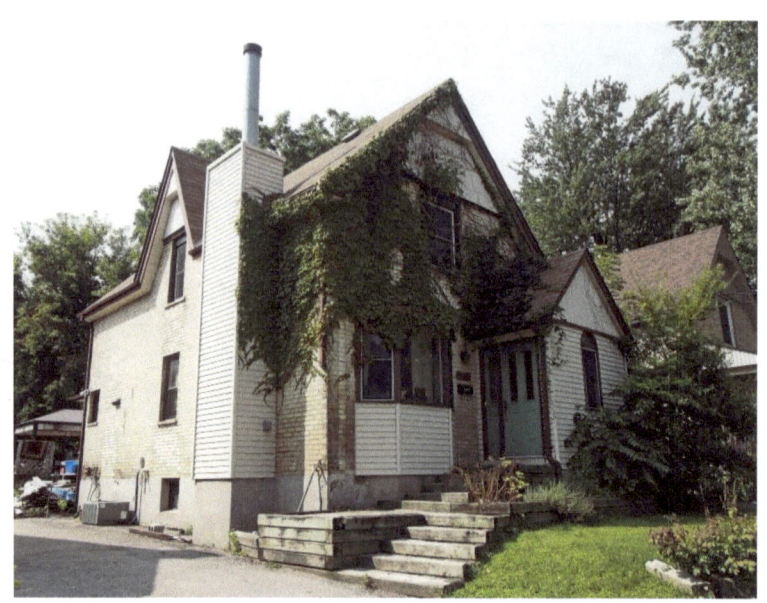

3983 Hamilton Road – Gothic Revival

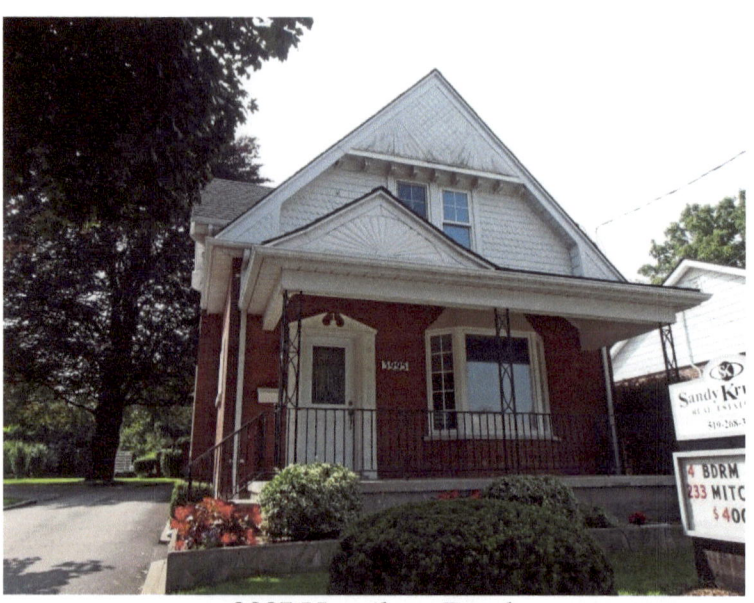

3995 Hamilton Road

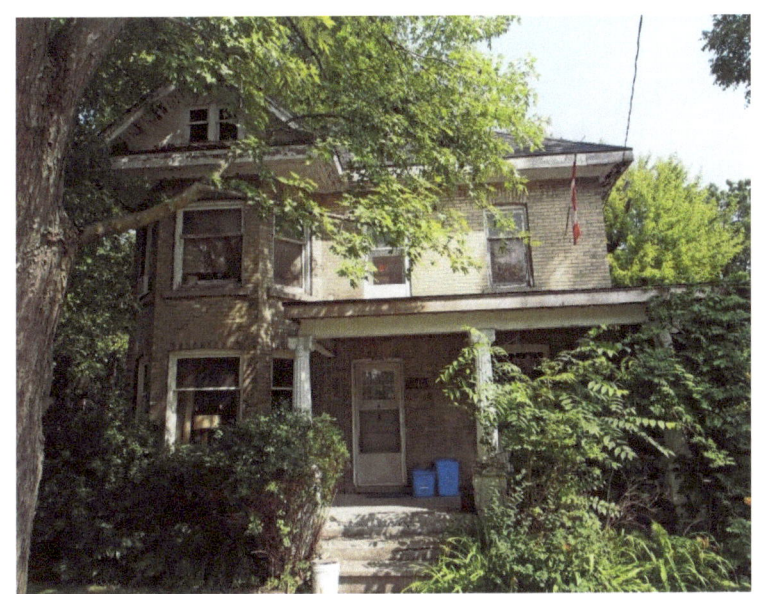

4010 Hamilton Road

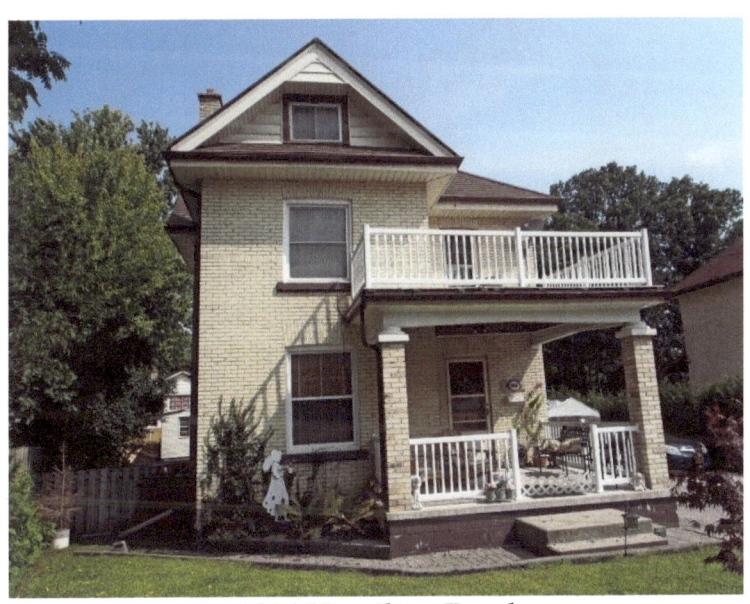

4016 Hamilton Road

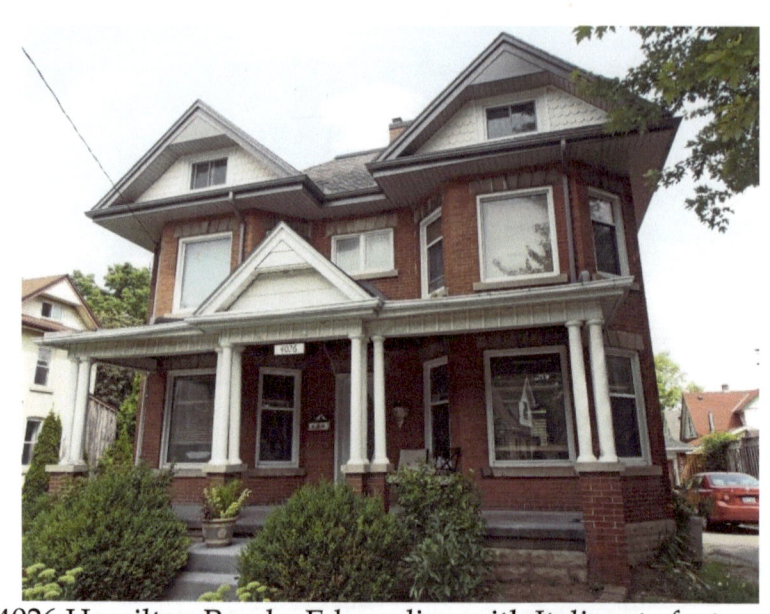

4026 Hamilton Road – Edwardian with Italianate features, two-storey bay window, pediment

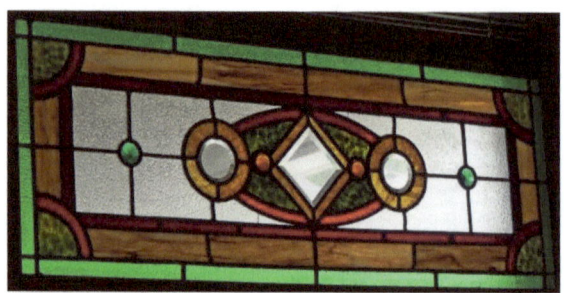

Stained glass

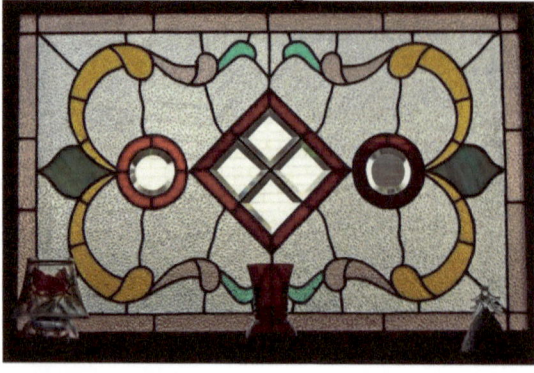

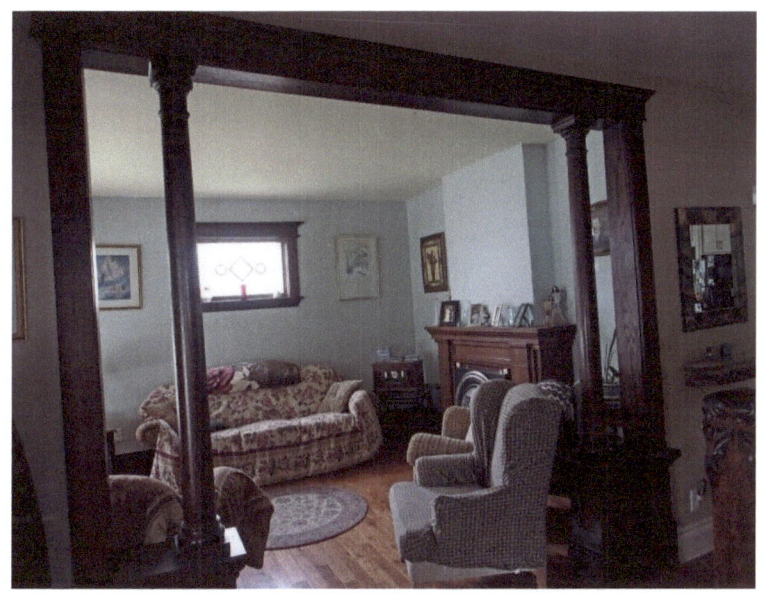

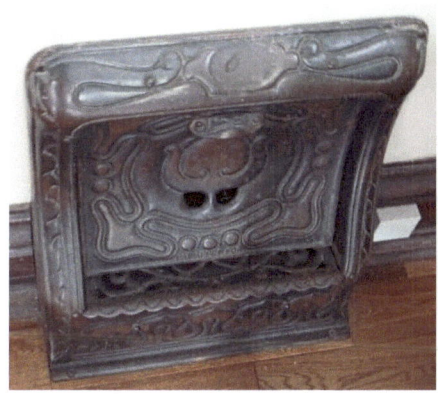

Original vent cover – now
Cold air return

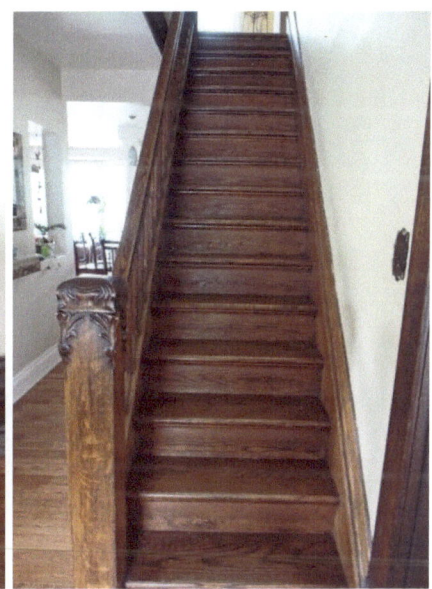

Original stairs and carving

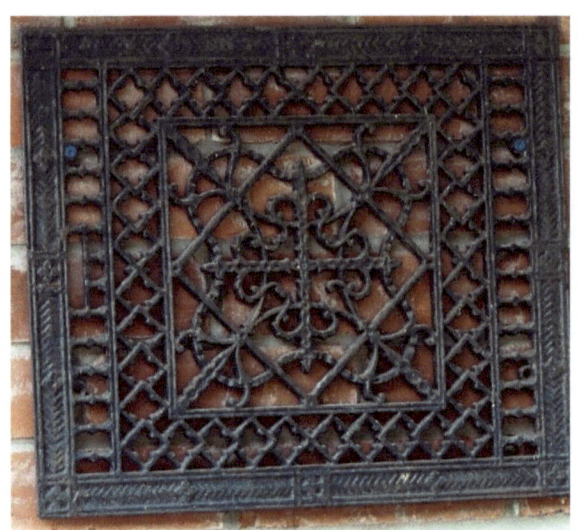

Vent cover – now wall hanging

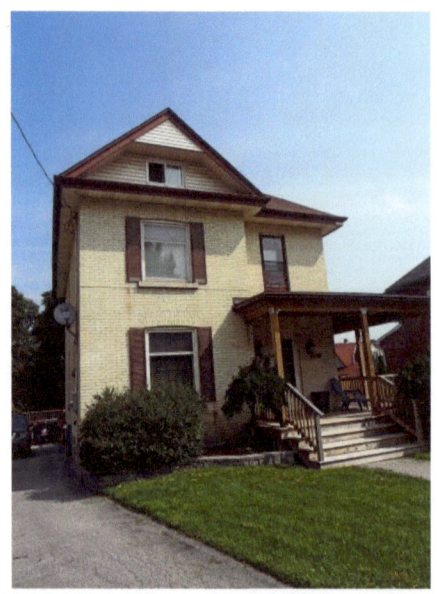

4020 Hamilton Road, Edwardian

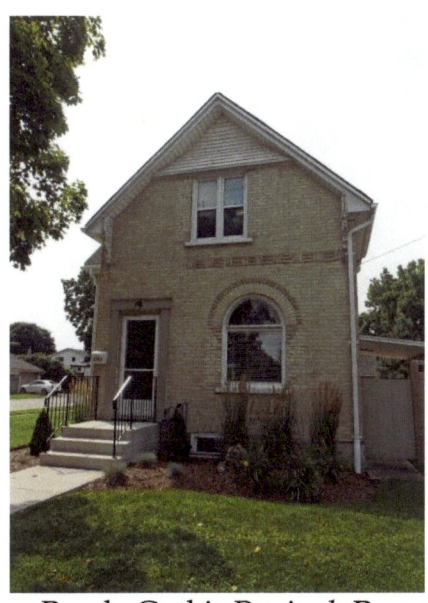

4101 Hamilton Road , Gothic Revival, Romanesque style
window arch, decorative brickwork

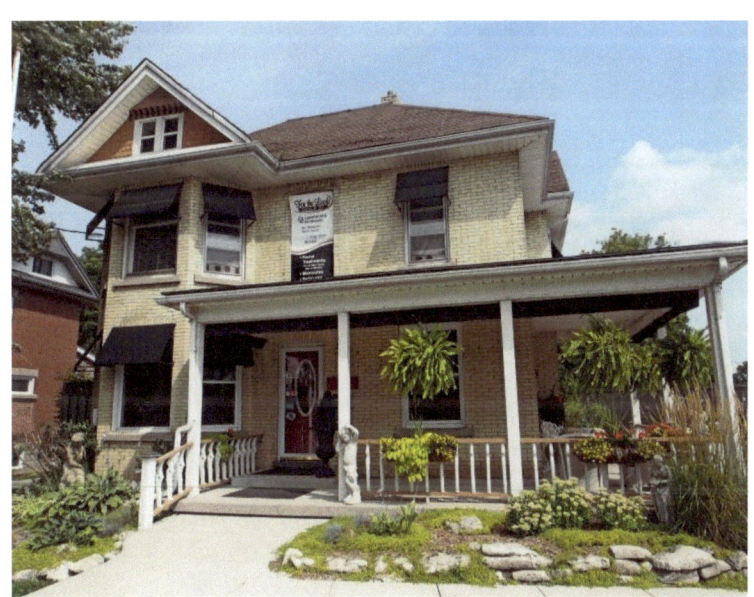

Hamilton Road – Edwardian/Italianate,
wraparound verandah

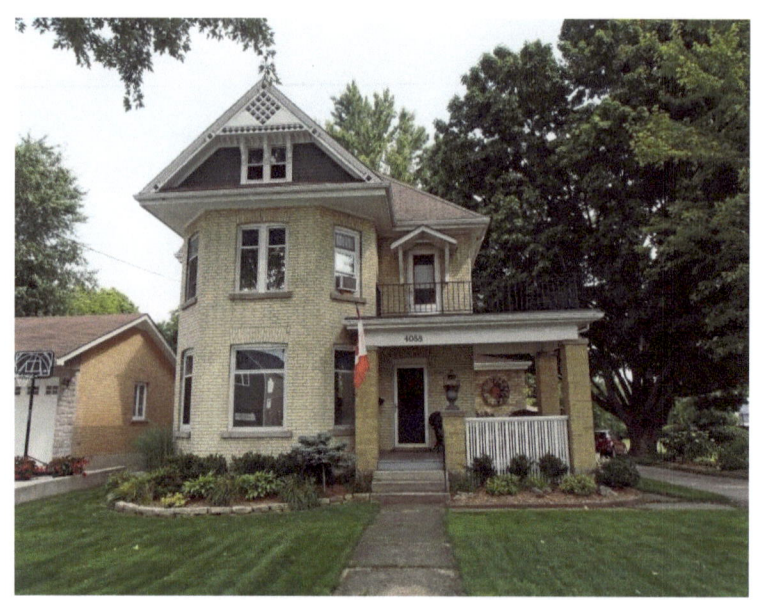

4088 Hamilton Road – Edwardian
with two-and-a-half storey tower-like bay

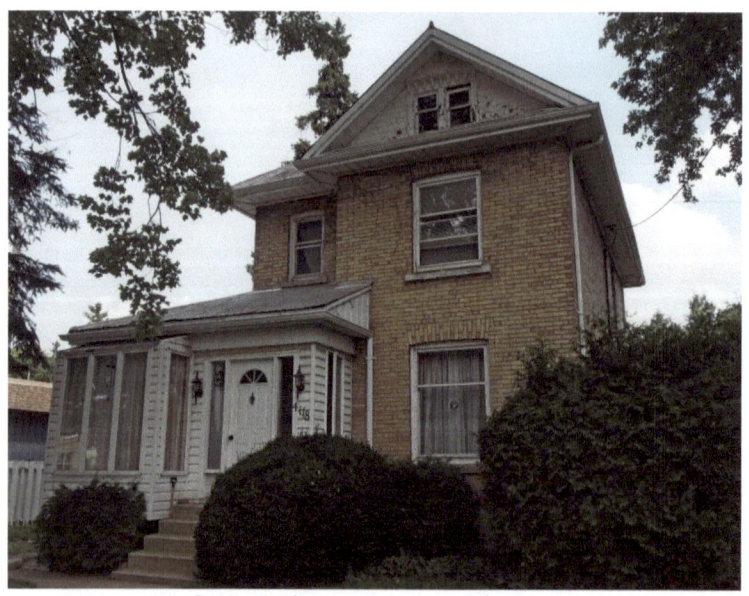

4118 Hamilton Road – Edwardian

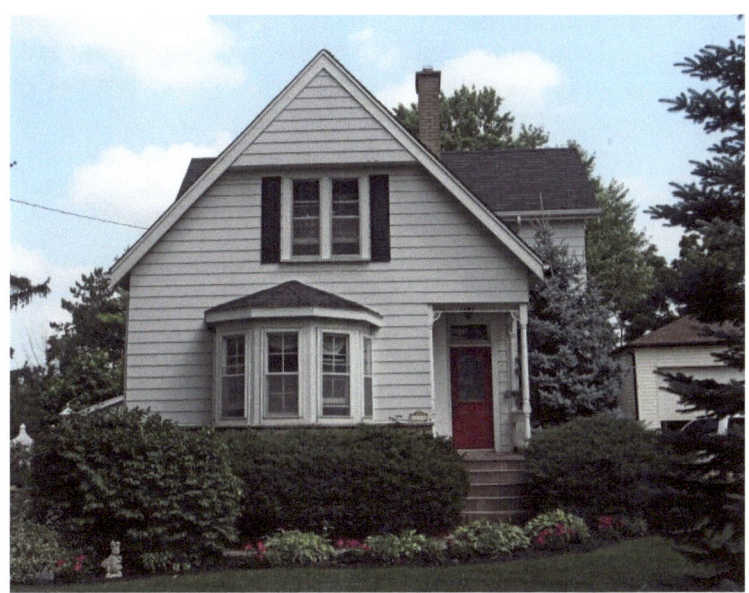

4124 Hamilton Road – Gothic Revival

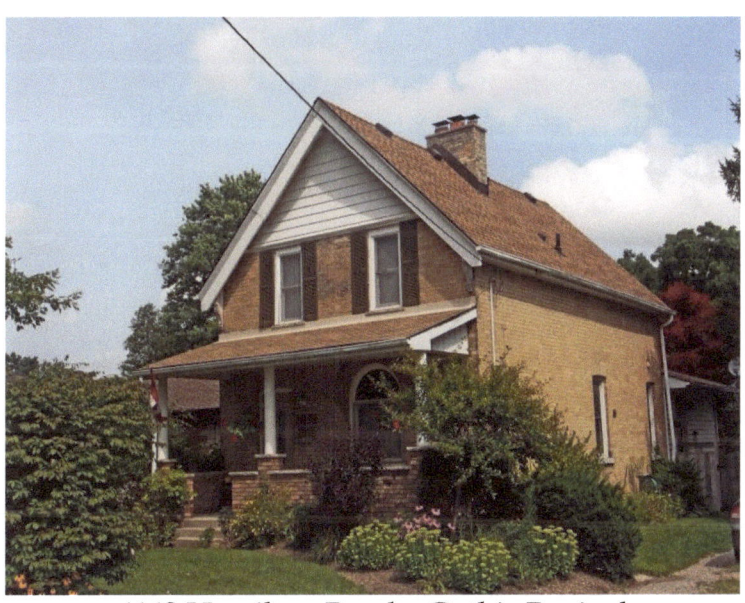

4142 Hamilton Road – Gothic Revival

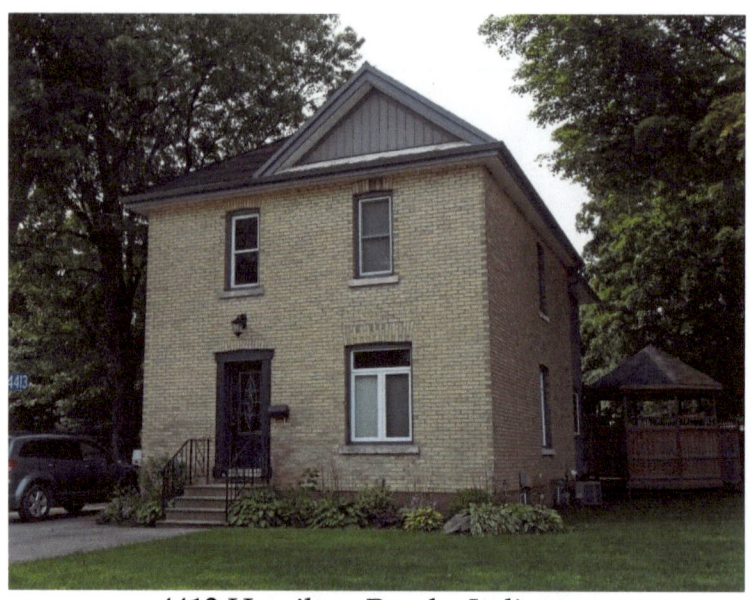

4413 Hamilton Road – Italianate

Mossley

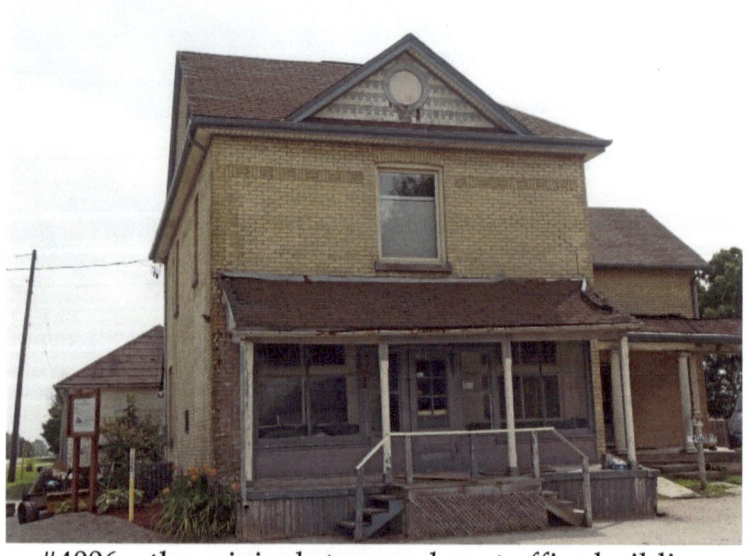

#4006 – the original store and post office building

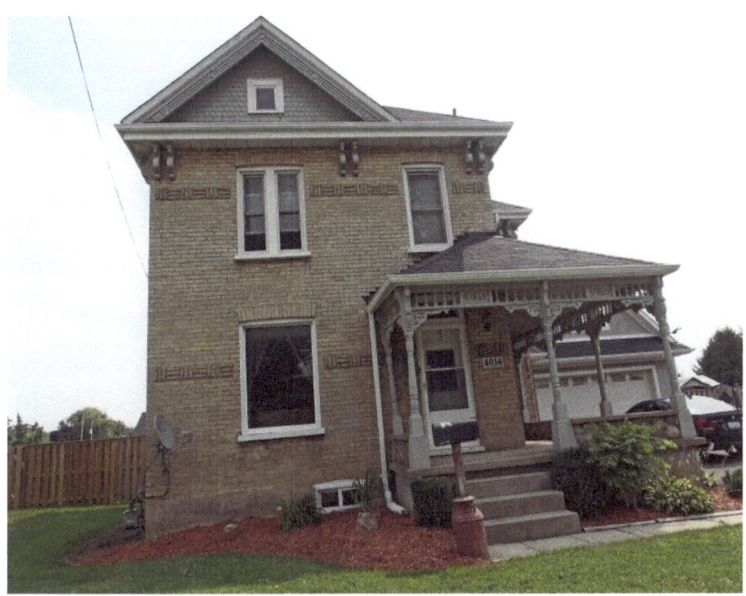

#4014 – Edwardian, cornice brackets

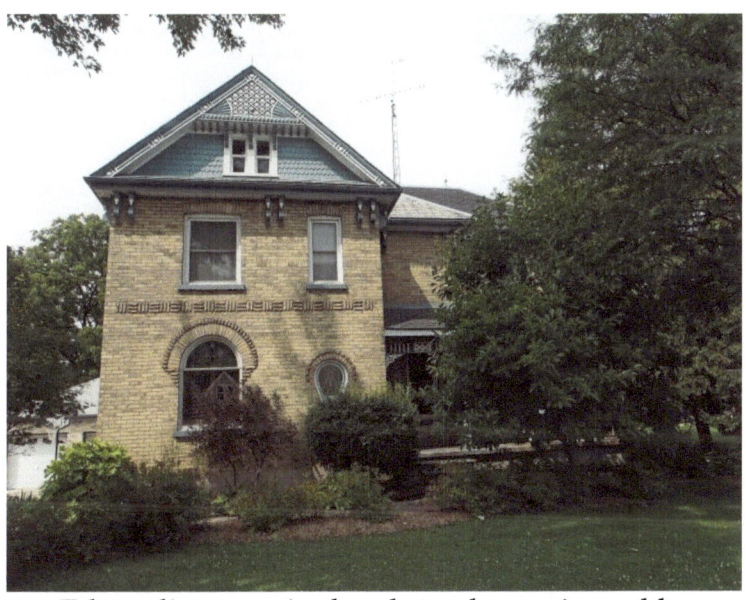

Edwardian, cornice brackets, decorative gable,
Romanesque style window arches

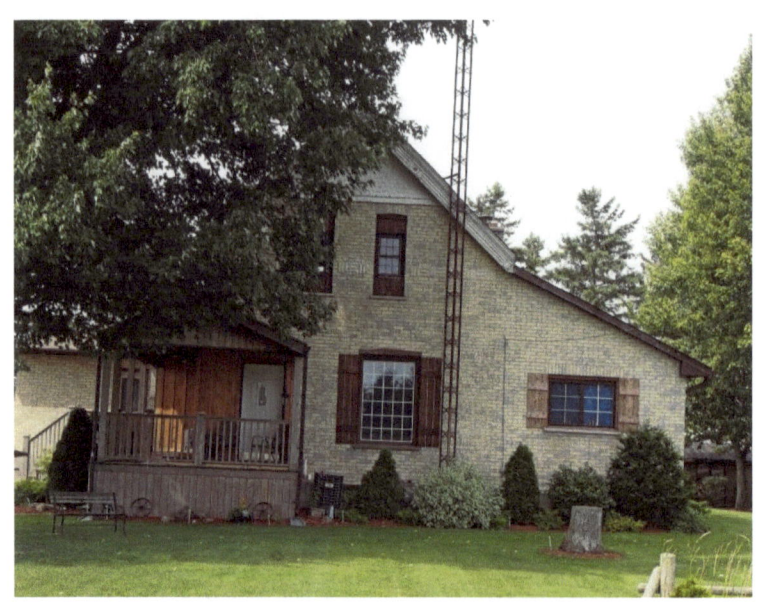

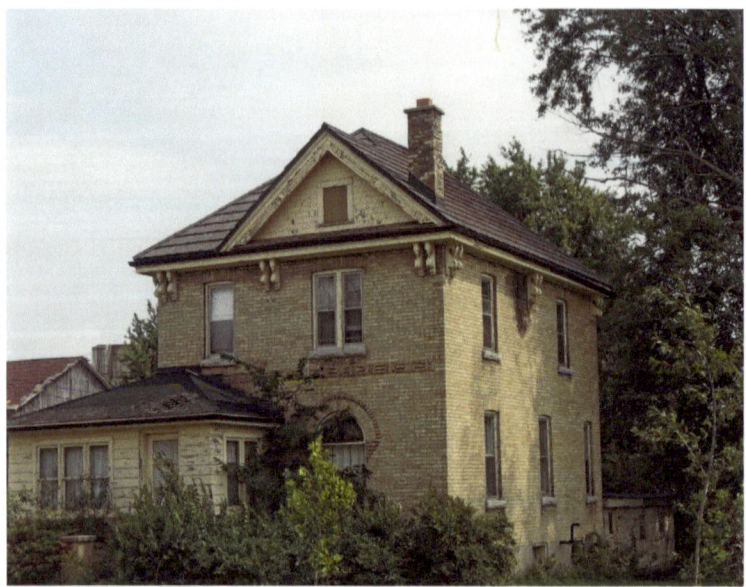

Cornice brackets

Harrietsville

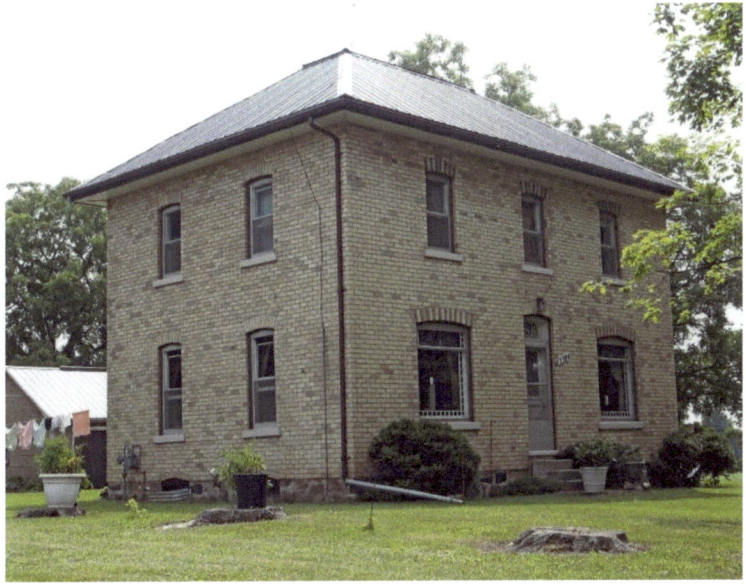

5384 Elgin Road -1899 – Italianate, hipped roof

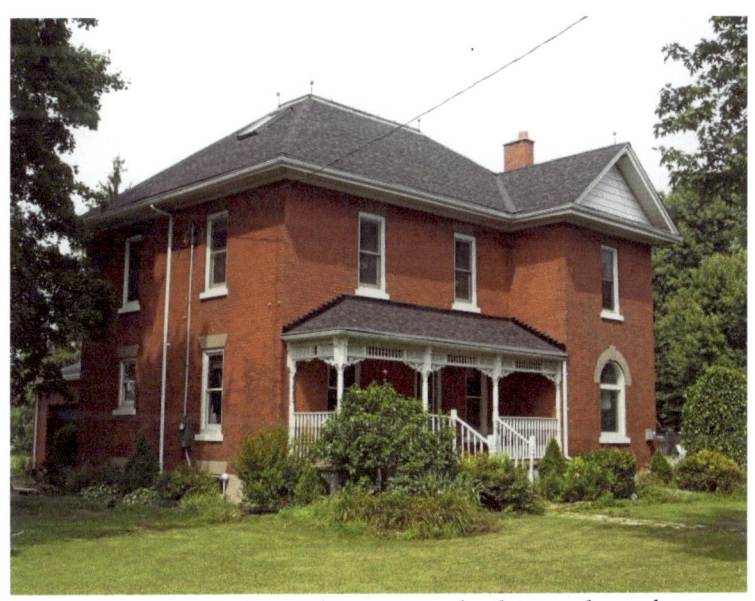

Elgin Road – Italianate style, hipped roof

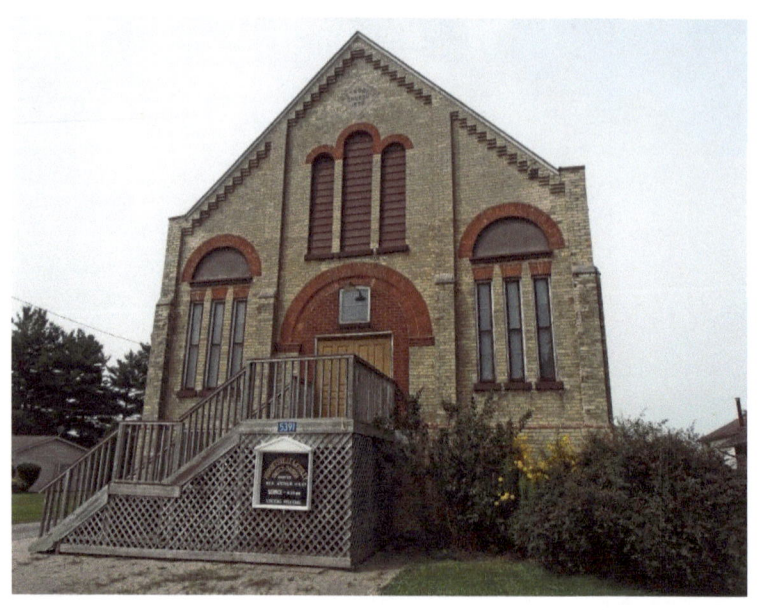

5391 Elgin Road – Harrietsville-Mossley United Church – former Methodist Church – 1896 – Gothic Revival

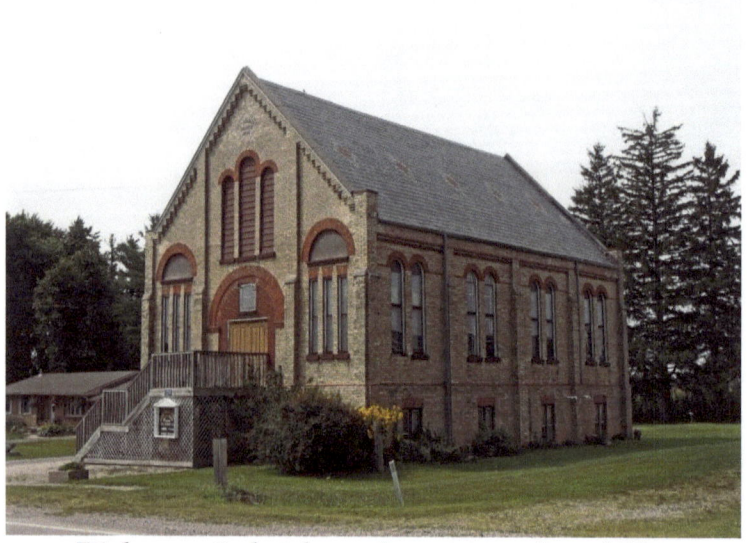

Dichromatic brick work, patterned roof tiles

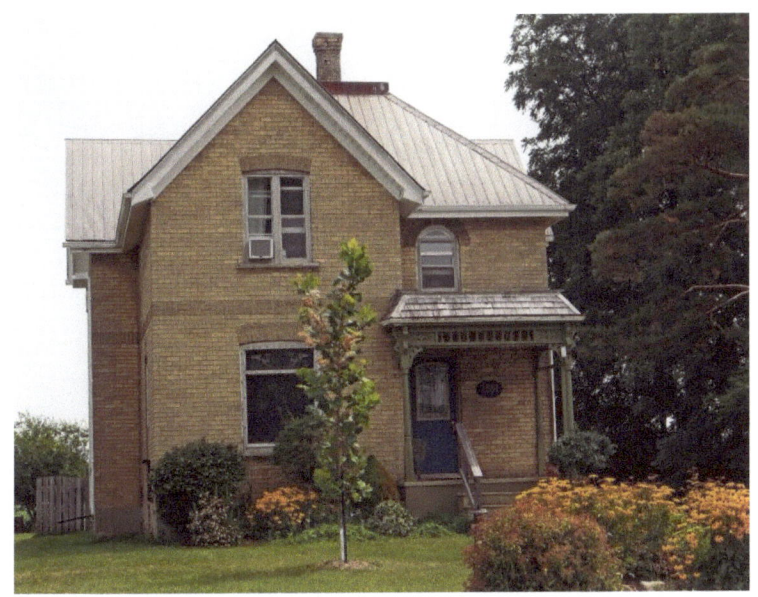

Elgin Road – Gothic Revival style

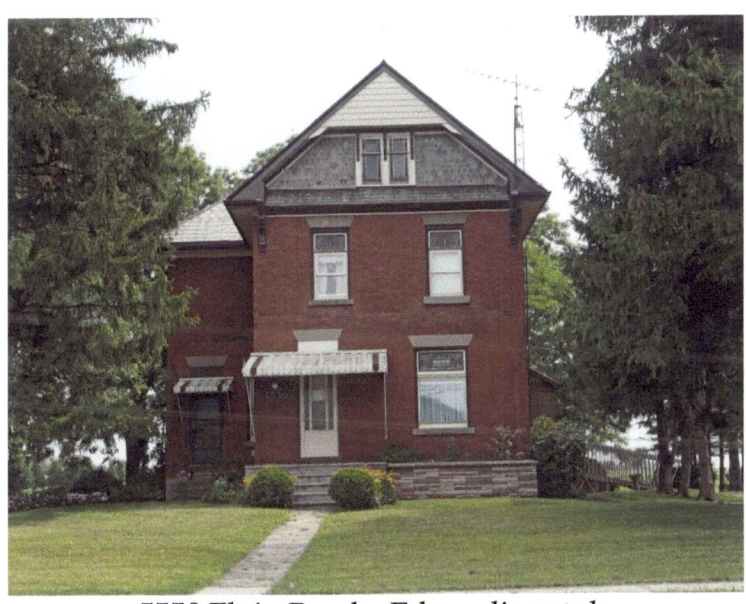

5550 Elgin Road – Edwardian style

Lyons

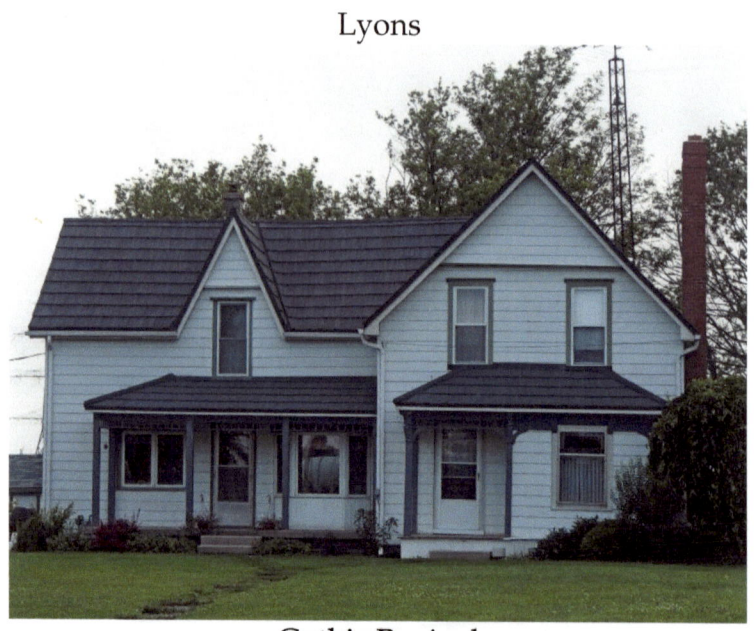

Gothic Revival

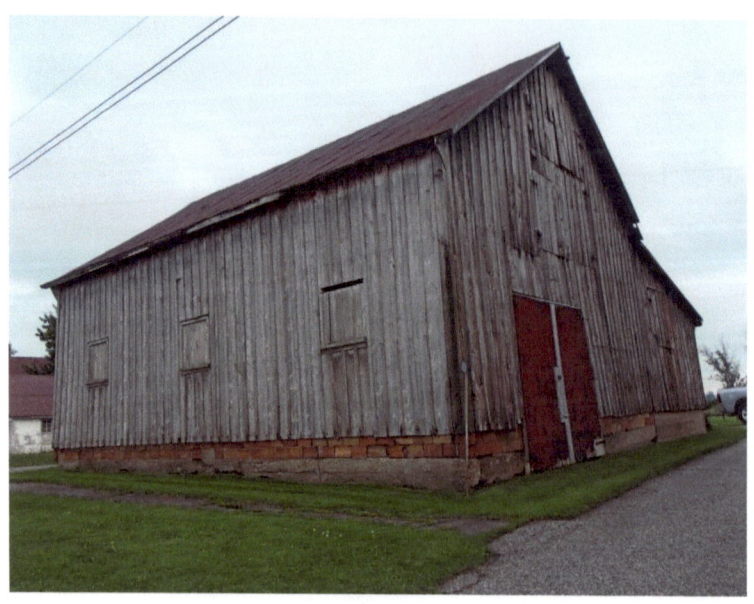

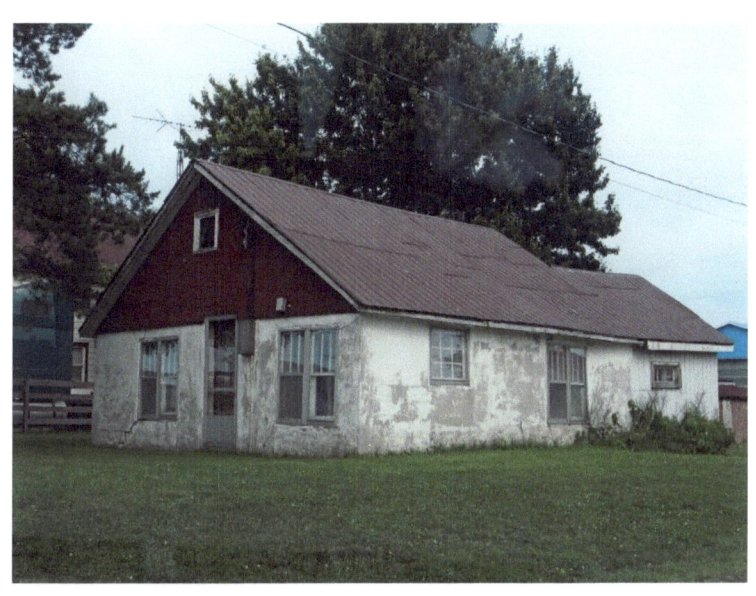

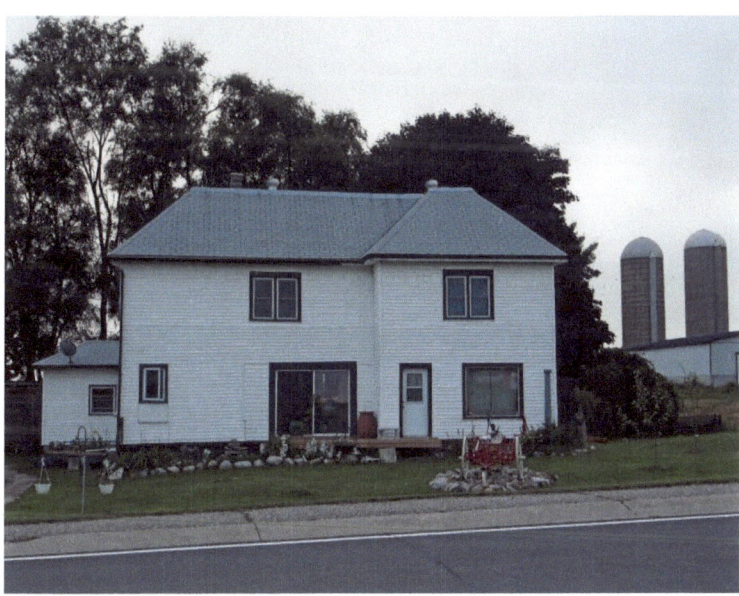

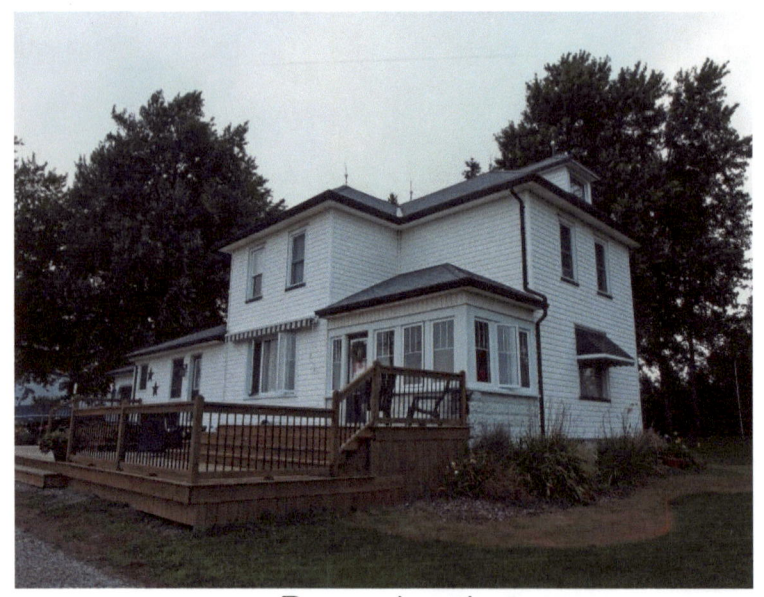

Dormer in attic

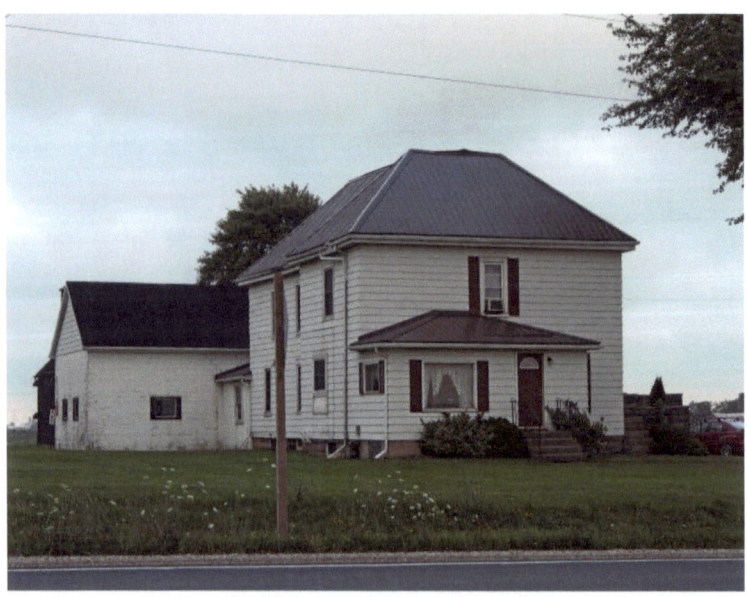

Italianate, hipped roof

Port Bruce

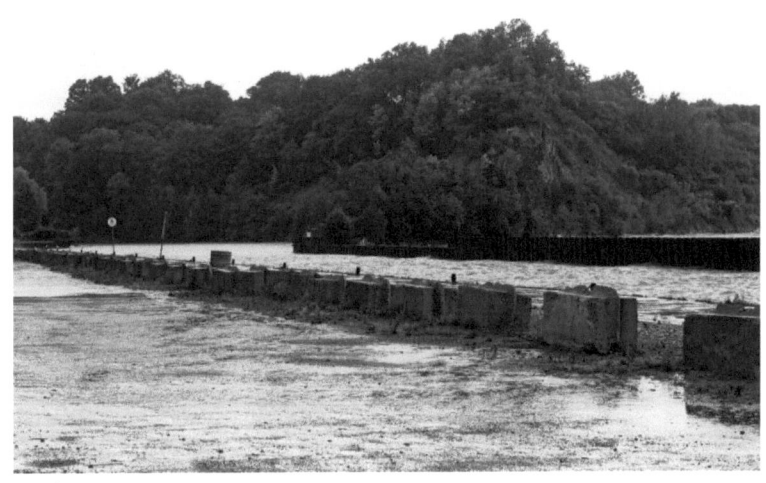

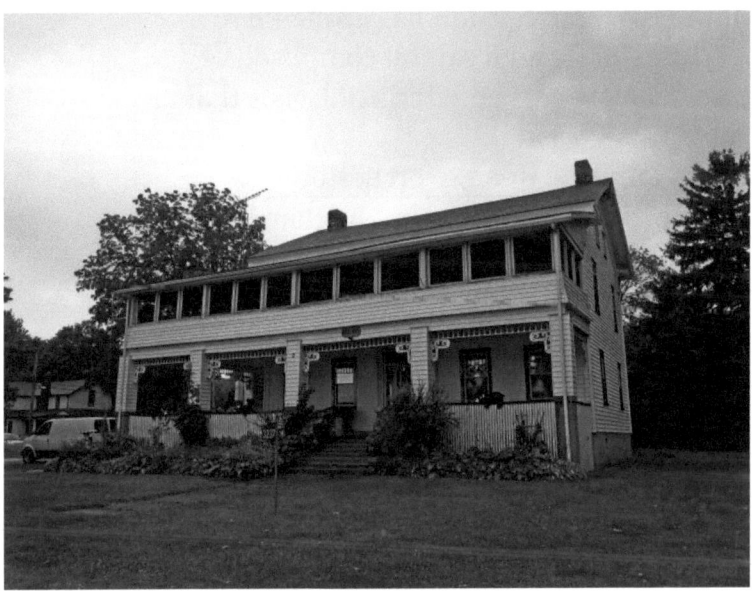

#3237 – built in 1854

Architectural Terms

Belvedere: (from the Italian "beautiful view") an architectural feature on a roof, in a garden or on a terrace that gives a beautiful view. Example: 31 Mill Road, Dorchester	
Brackets: a decorative or weight-bearing structural element which forms a right angle with one side against a wall and the other under a projecting surface such as an eave or roof. Example: Mossley	
Buttress: a masonry structure built against or projecting from a wall which serves to support or reinforce the wall. In Canadian architecture, they are sometimes used for decoration. Example: Harrietsville-Mossley United Church	
Capital: The uppermost finish or decoration on a column. An Ionic column has a small base, a thin elegant shaft, and a capital composed of volutes which are carved whirls or twists that take the form of a scroll. Example: Hamilton Road, Dorchester	
Cornice: originally the wooden overhang of the roof. With the use of stone, brick, iron and steel, the cornice is any projecting shelf at the top of a ceiling or roof. They can be very decorative. Example: 4020 Hamilton Road, Dorchester	
Dichromatic brickwork: the use of two colours of brick, tile or slate to decorate a façade. Example: Harrietsville-Mossley United Church	

Dormer: (French for "sleep") a gable end window that pierces through the plane of a sloping roof surface to create usable space in the top floor or attic of a building by adding headroom. Example: 3937 Hamilton Road, Dorchester	
Gable: the triangular portion of a wall between the edges of a sloping roof. Example: Mossley	
Hipped Roof: a roof where all sides slope downwards to the walls with no gables. Example: 3944 Hamilton Road, Dorchester	
Lancet Window: a tall, narrow window with a pointed arch at its top. Example: Harrietsville-Mossley United Church	
Pediment: a triangular section above the horizontal structure (entablature), typically supported by columns. The inside of the triangle is called the tympanum. Example: 3969 Hamilton Road, Dorchester	
Vergeboard: also called bargeboards – hang from the projecting end of a roof and are often elaborately carved and ornamented. Example: 15 Bridge Street, Dorchester	

Edwardian, 1900-1930 – This style bridges the ornate and elaborate styles of the Victorian era and the simplified styles of the 20th century. Balanced facades, simple roof lines, dormer windows, large front porches, and smooth brick surfaces are its characteristics. Example: Mossley	
Georgian, before 1860 – This style began with the British King Georges in the 18th century. These buildings have balanced facades around a central door, medium-pitched gable roofs, and small paned windows. Example: 31 Mill Road, Dorchester	
Gothic Revival, 1830-1890 – These decorative buildings have sharply-pitched gables with highly detailed vergeboards, pointed-arch window openings, and dichromatic brickwork. It is a common style in Ontario. Example: Lyons	
Italianate, 1850-1900 – It has wide-bracketed eaves, belvederes, wrap-around verandahs. Example: 5384 Elgin Road, Harrietsville	
Romanesque Revival, 1880-1910 – This style hearkens back to medieval architecture of the 11th and 12th centuries with a heavy appearance, blocky towers and rounded arches. Romanesque style window arch Example: Mossley	